WRITING BOOK FOR KINDERGARTEN

Preschool Alphabet Workbook

Includes Motivational Quotes for Kids

WRITING BOOK FOR KINDERGARTEN
Preschool Alphabet Workbook

@2021 Andrea Clarke Pratt

This Book Belongs to:

EVERYTHING
YOU AN
IMAGINE
IS
POSSIBLE

Find And Circle The letter.

G Q A V X Z
A C B E S W
D T J H A L
C X M A N O

Acorn

Trace The Letter Then Write Your Own.

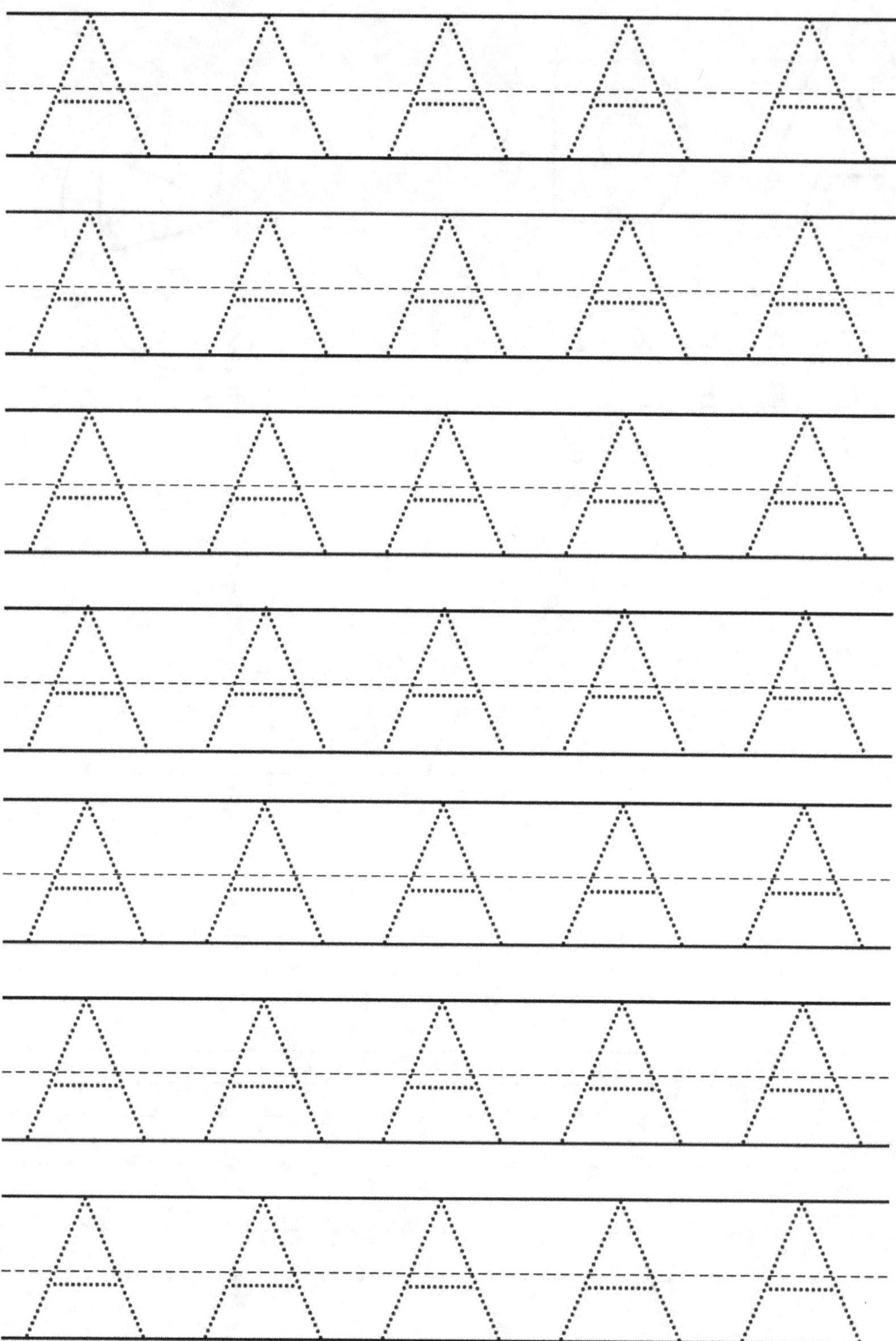

a a a a a a a a

a a a a a a a a

a a a a a a a a

a a a a a a a a

a a a a a a a a

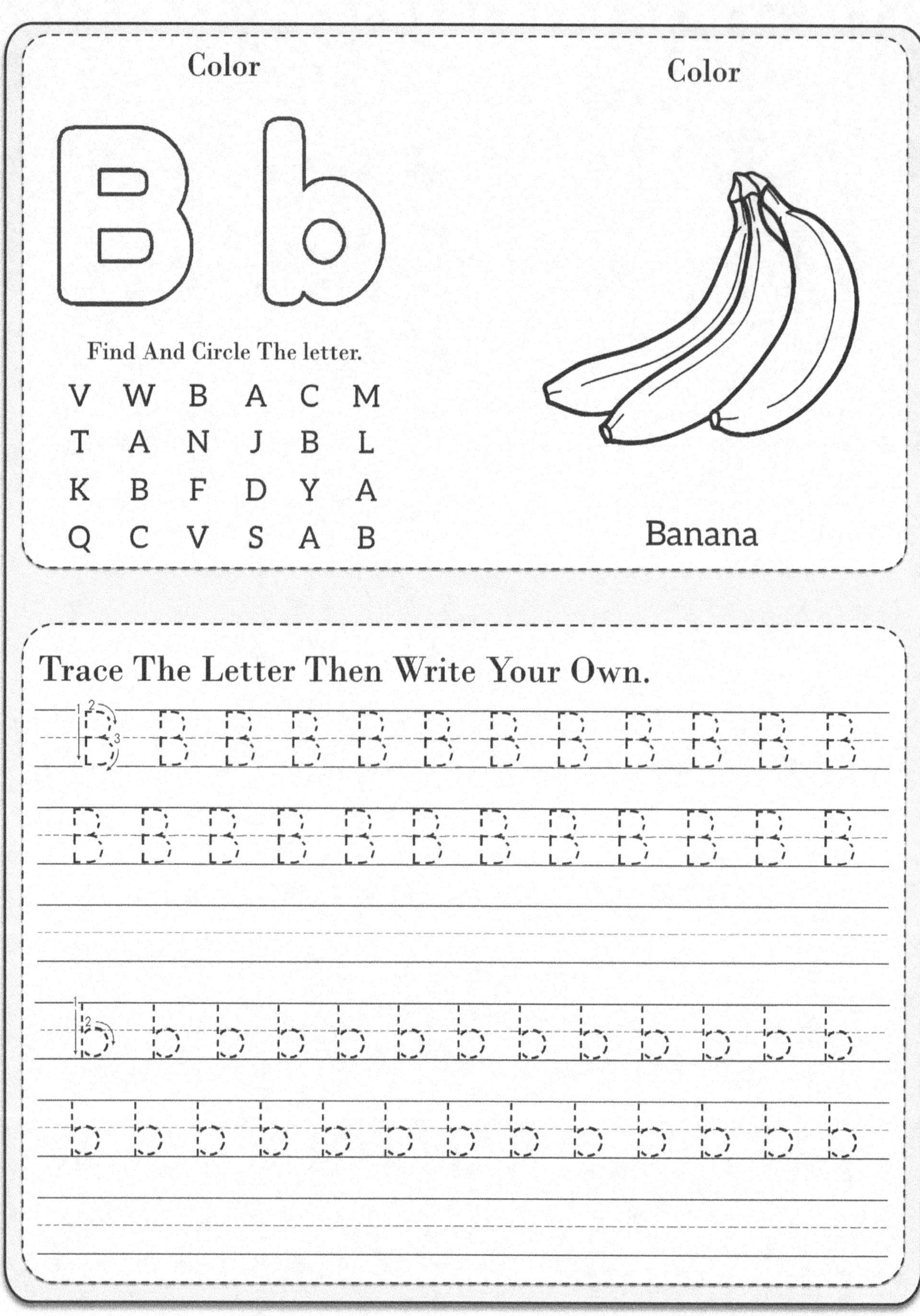

Trace The Letter Then Write Your Own.

B B B B B

B B B B B

B B B B B

B B B B B

B B B B B

B B B B B

B B B B B

EVERY
DAY
IS A
FRESH
START

C c

Find And Circle The letter.

C	Z	L	B	K	O
X	N	C	Y	A	T
Q	C	B	W	V	B
G	F	H	C	J	K

Cat

Trace The Letter Then Write Your Own.

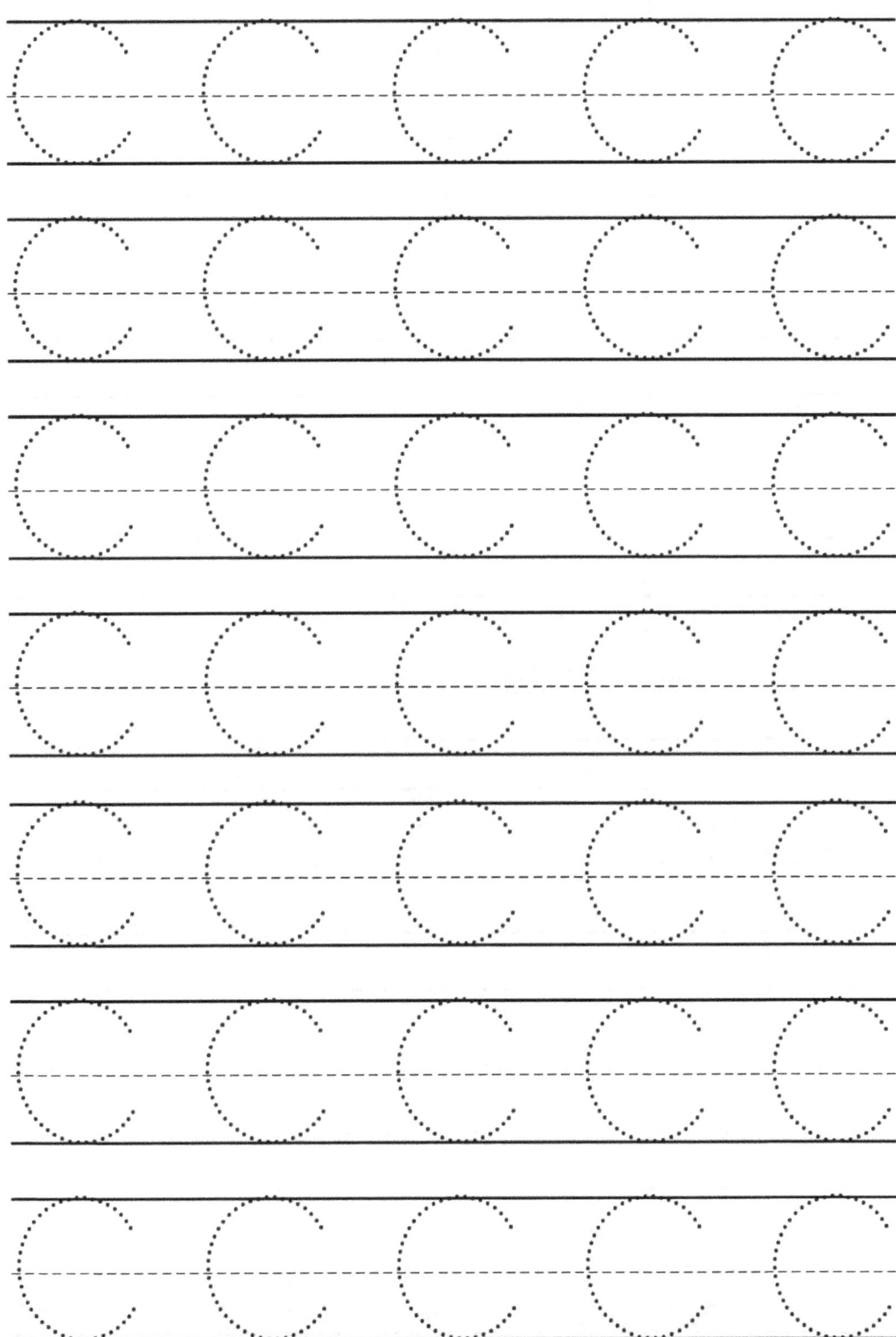

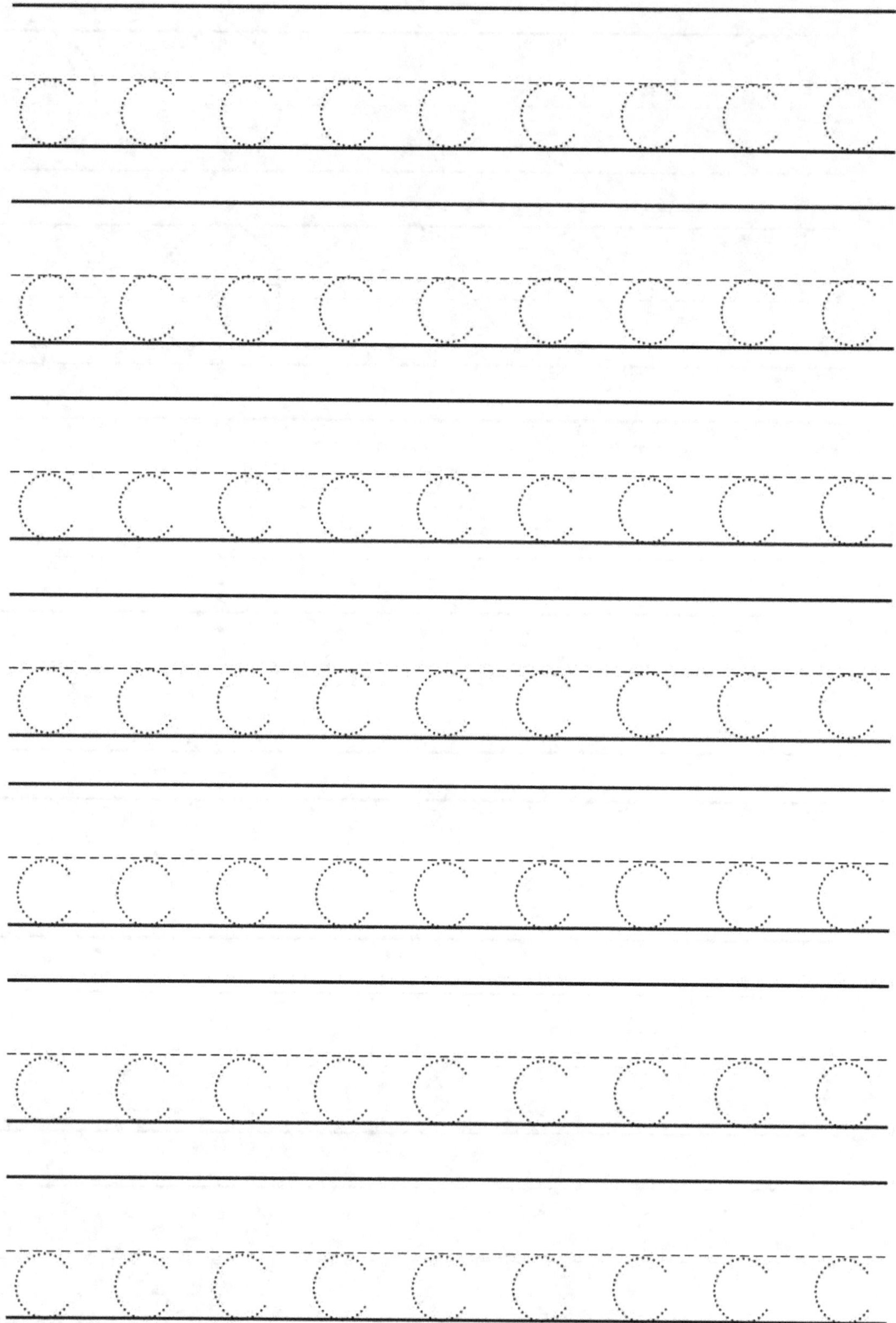

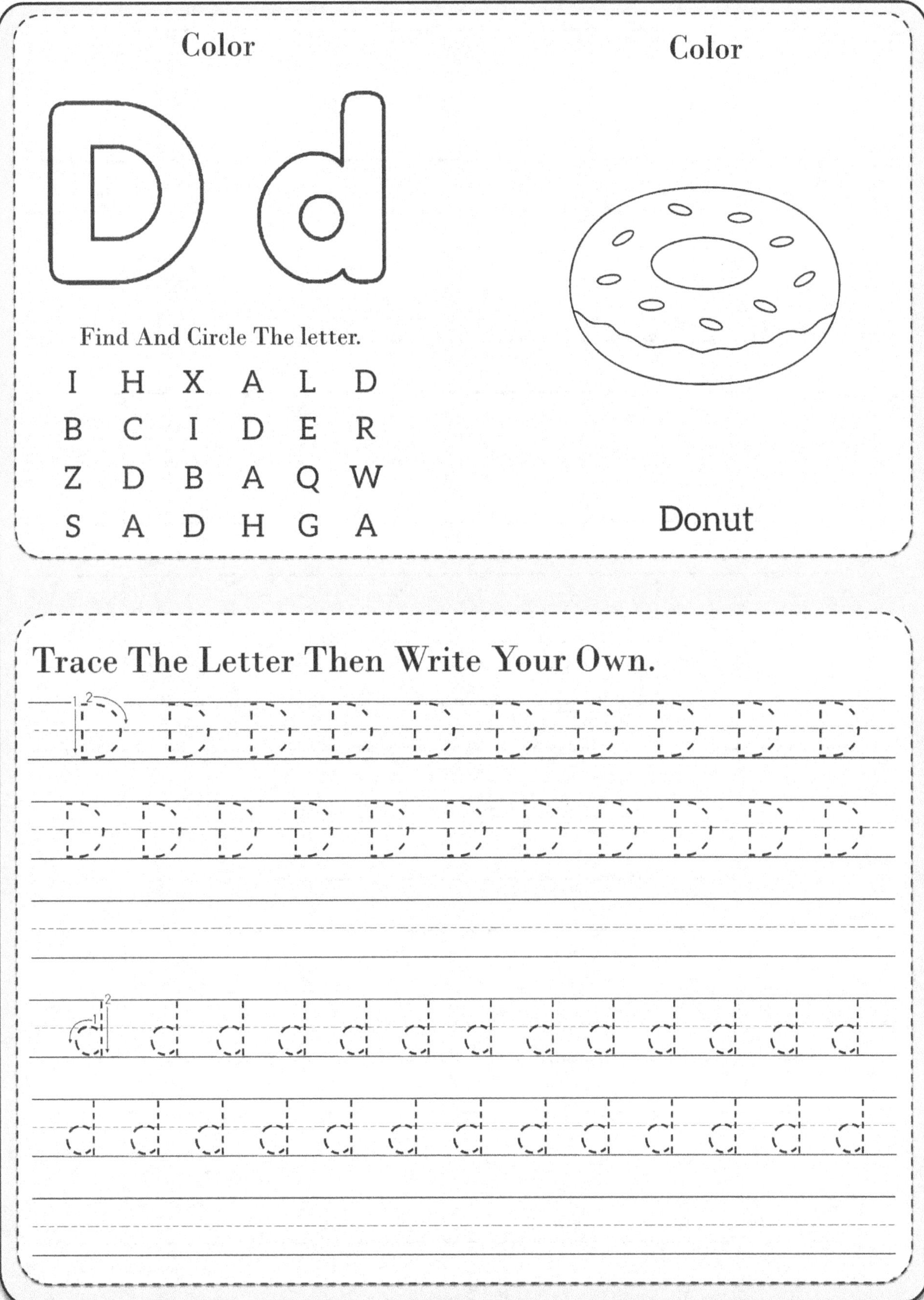

Color

Color

D d

Find And Circle The letter.

I H X A L D
B C I D E R
Z D B A Q W
S A D H G A

Donut

Trace The Letter Then Write Your Own.

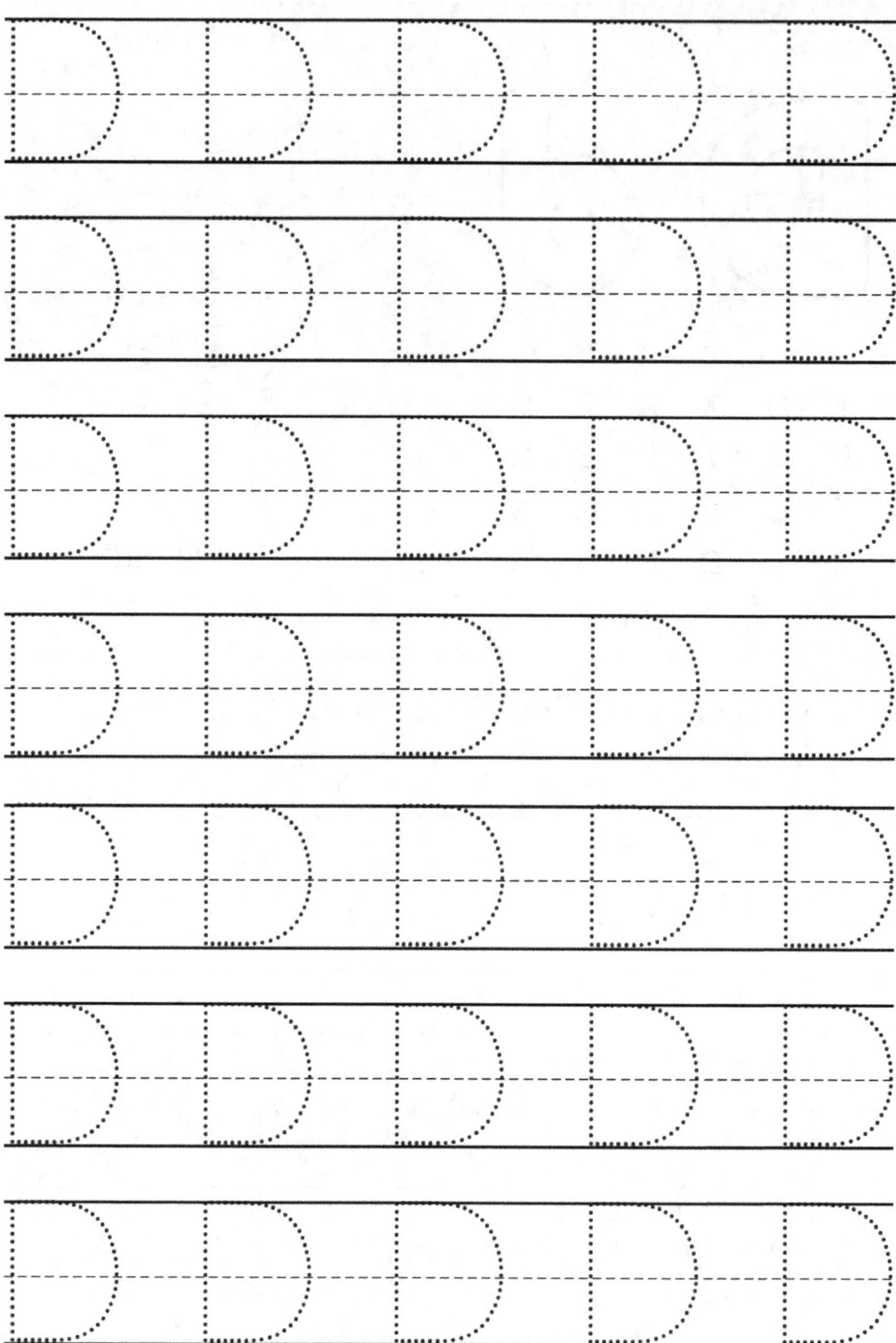

E e

Find And Circle The letter.

T	B	I	L	K	E
A	V	E	D	S	W
C	Q	B	N	E	N
E	M	J	I	X	Z

Eggplant

Trace The Letter Then Write Your Own.

e e e e e e e

e e e e e e e

e e e e e e e

e e e e e e e

e e e e e e e

e e e e e e e

IF YOU
DREAM IT
YOU
CAN
DO IT

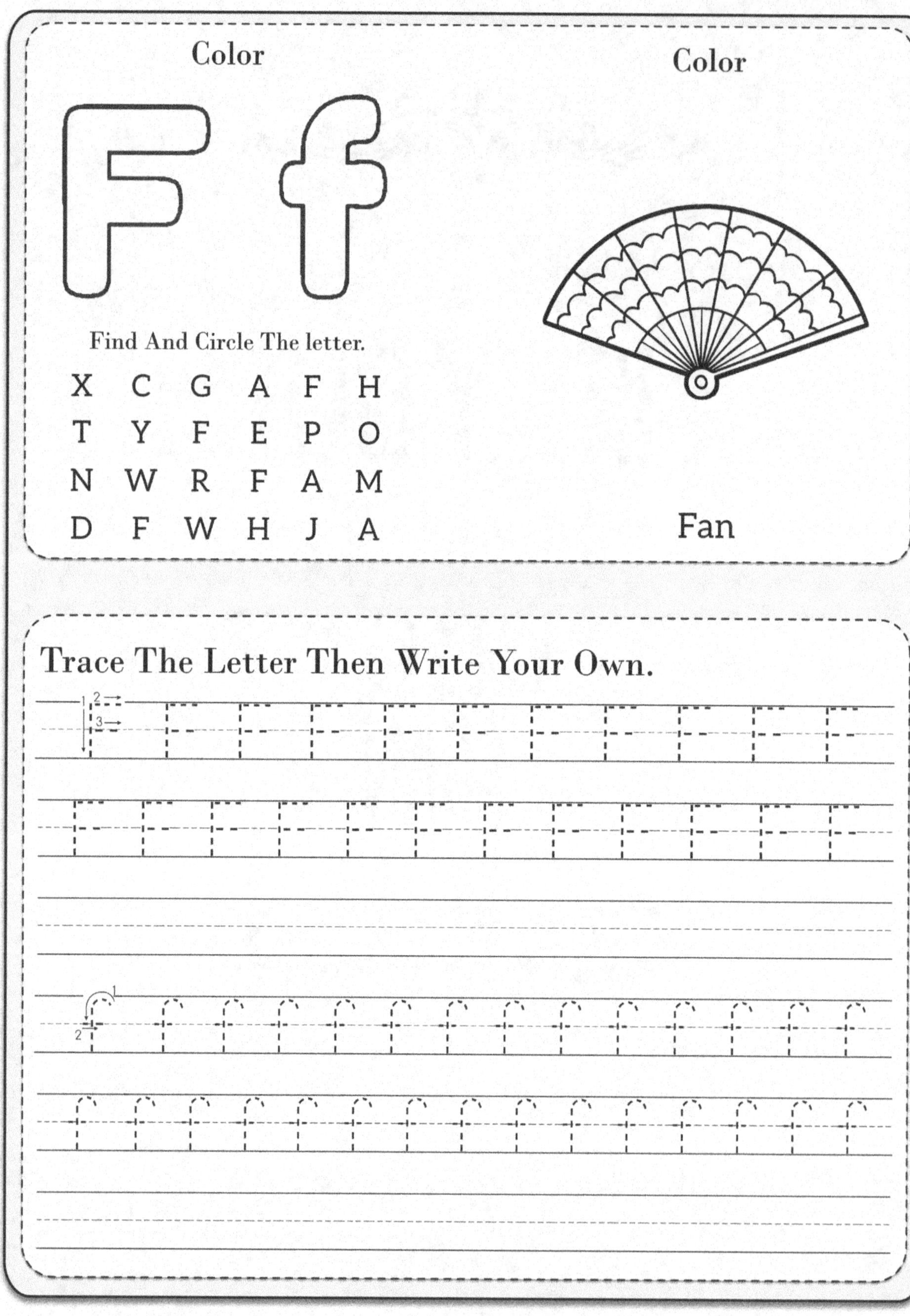

Find And Circle The letter.

X C G A F H
T Y F E P O
N W R F A M
D F W H J A

Fan

Trace The Letter Then Write Your Own.

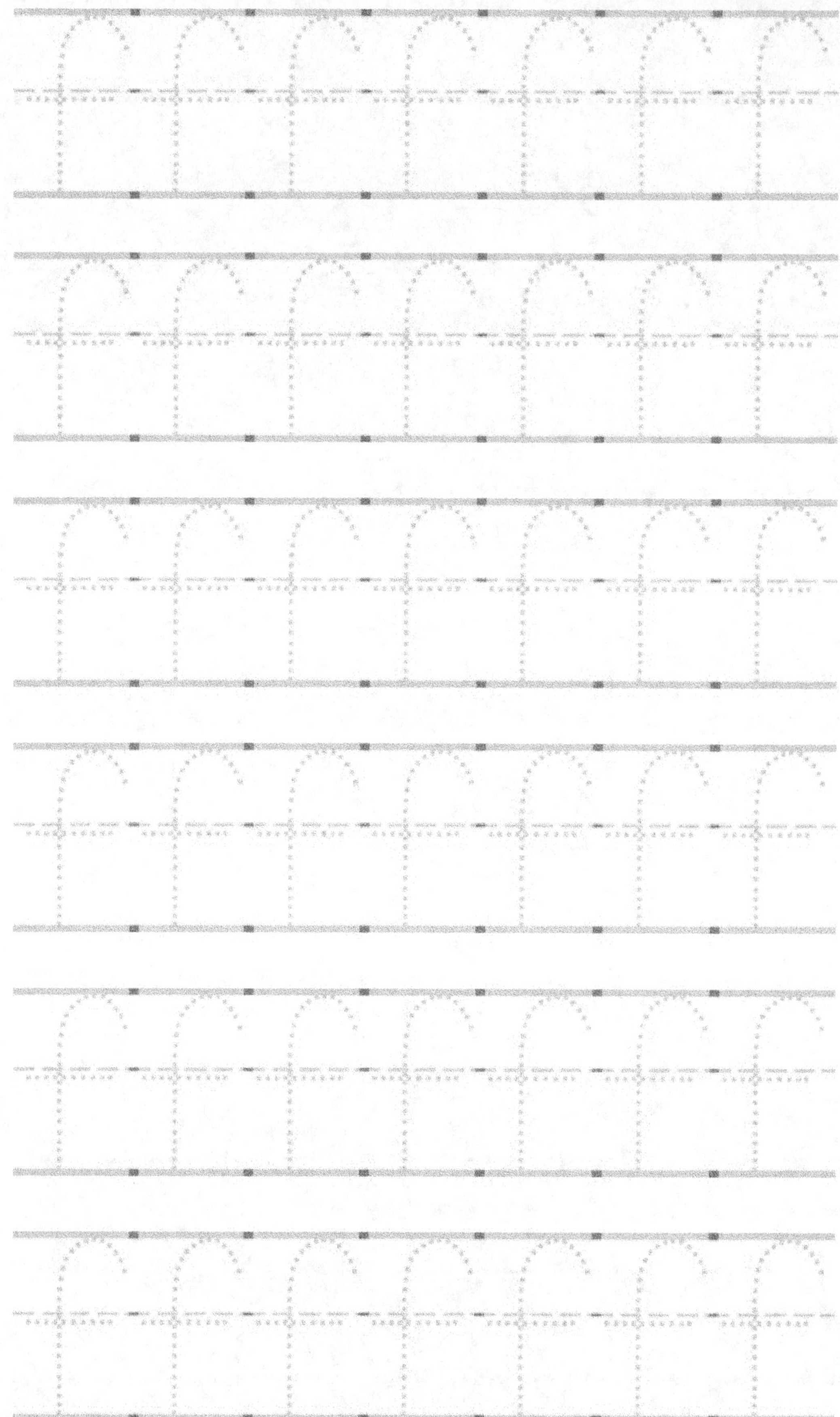

G g

Find And Circle The letter.

R	A	H	L	G	K
M	I	G	P	O	S
R	T	Y	U	X	G
Z	G	C	V	N	J

Giraffe

Trace The Letter Then Write Your Own.

H h

Find And Circle The letter.

Y	H	U	Q	T	W
Z	X	H	C	V	A
B	N	M	H	L	K
J	G	F	D	H	S

Hen

Trace The Letter Then Write Your Own.

IF YOU
PUT IN
the work,
THE
result
WILL COME

Ii

Find And Circle The letter.

Q	T	E	I	Y	R
I	S	D	F	G	A
H	J	K	L	N	I
W	A	I	V	C	P

Trace The Letter Then Write Your Own.

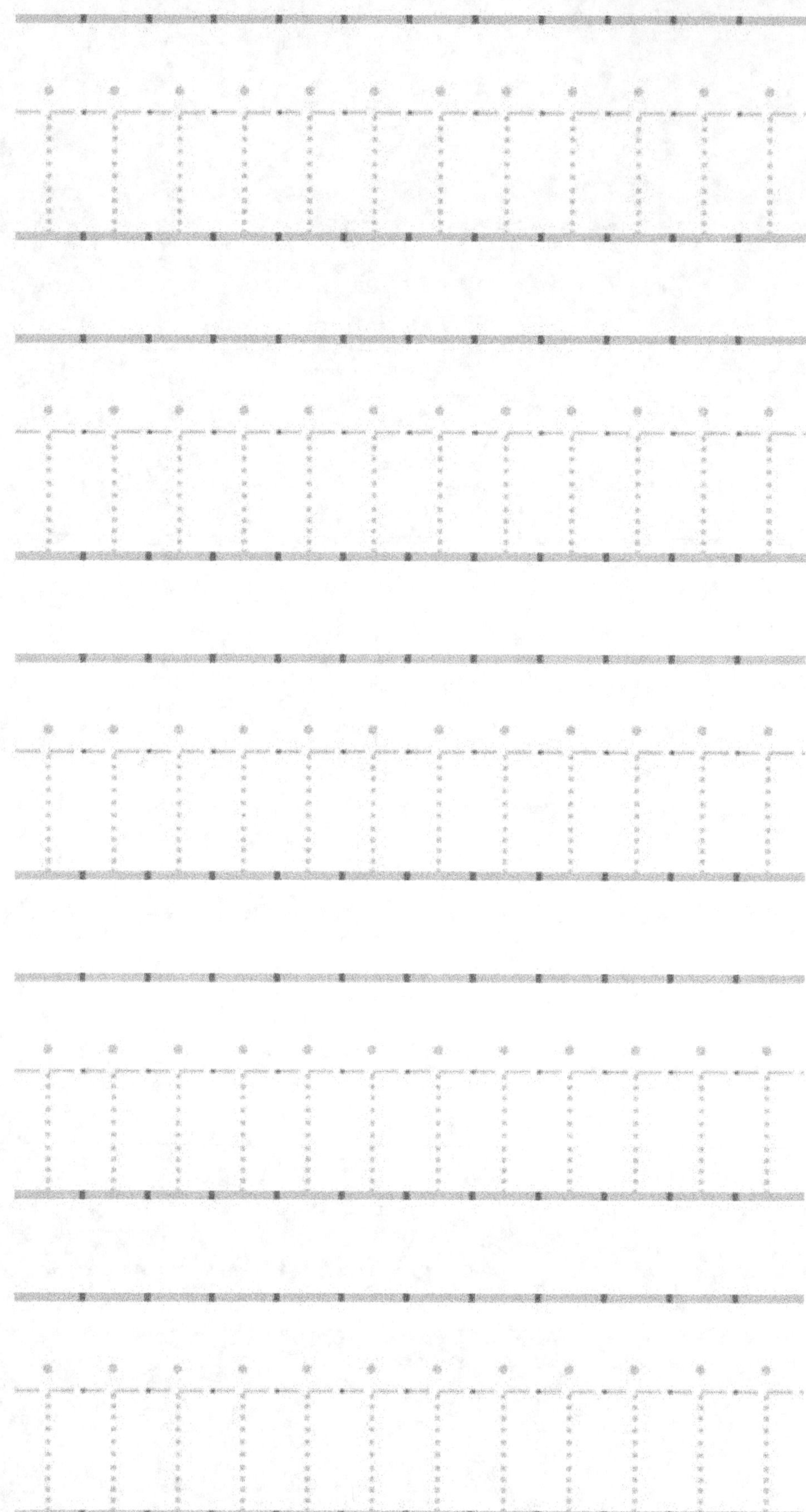

Color
Color
J j
Find And Circle The letter.
I B Q J F Q
J T R E W S
F G J H A K
L J U V M A
Jellyfish
Trace The Letter Then Write Your Own.

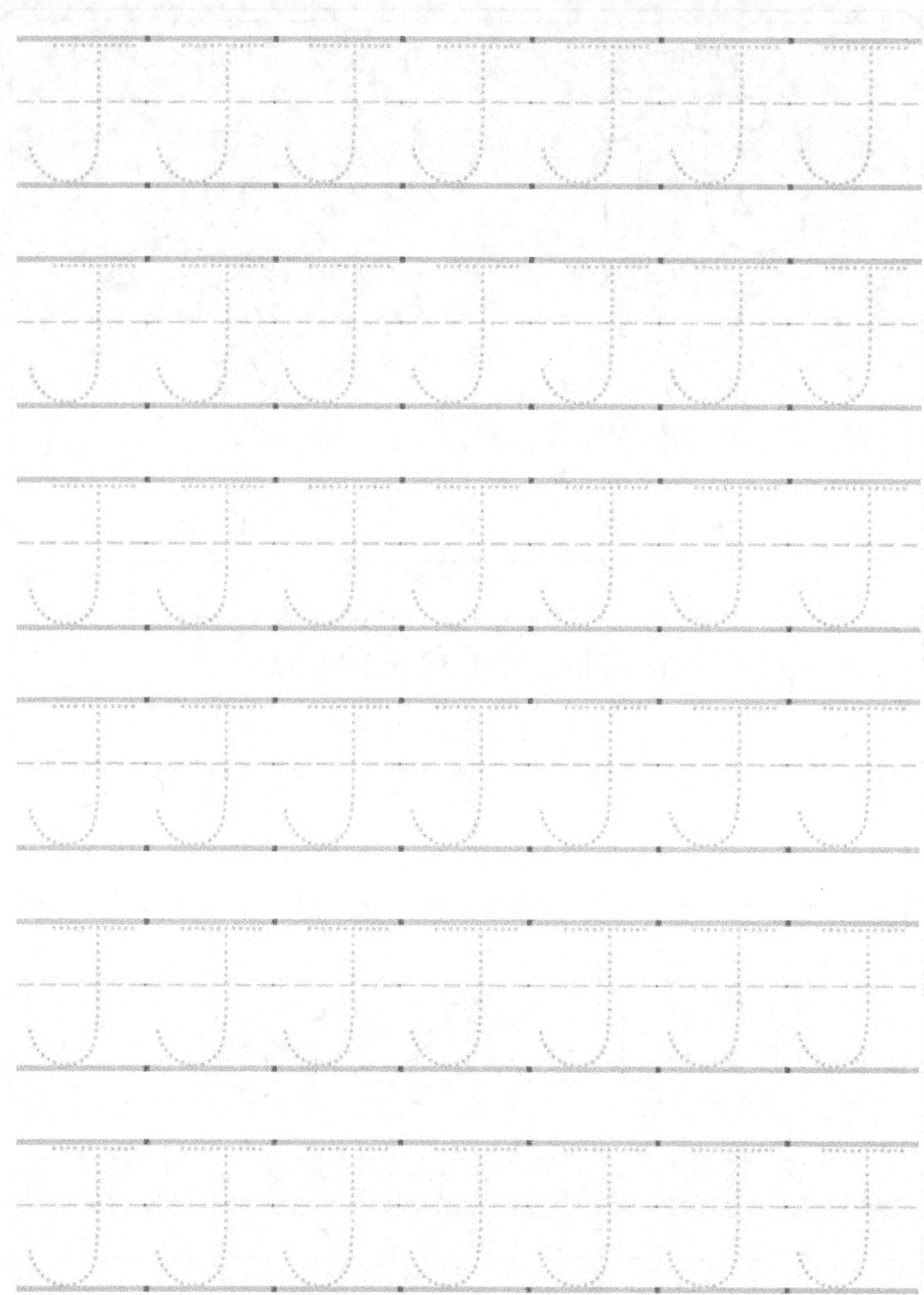

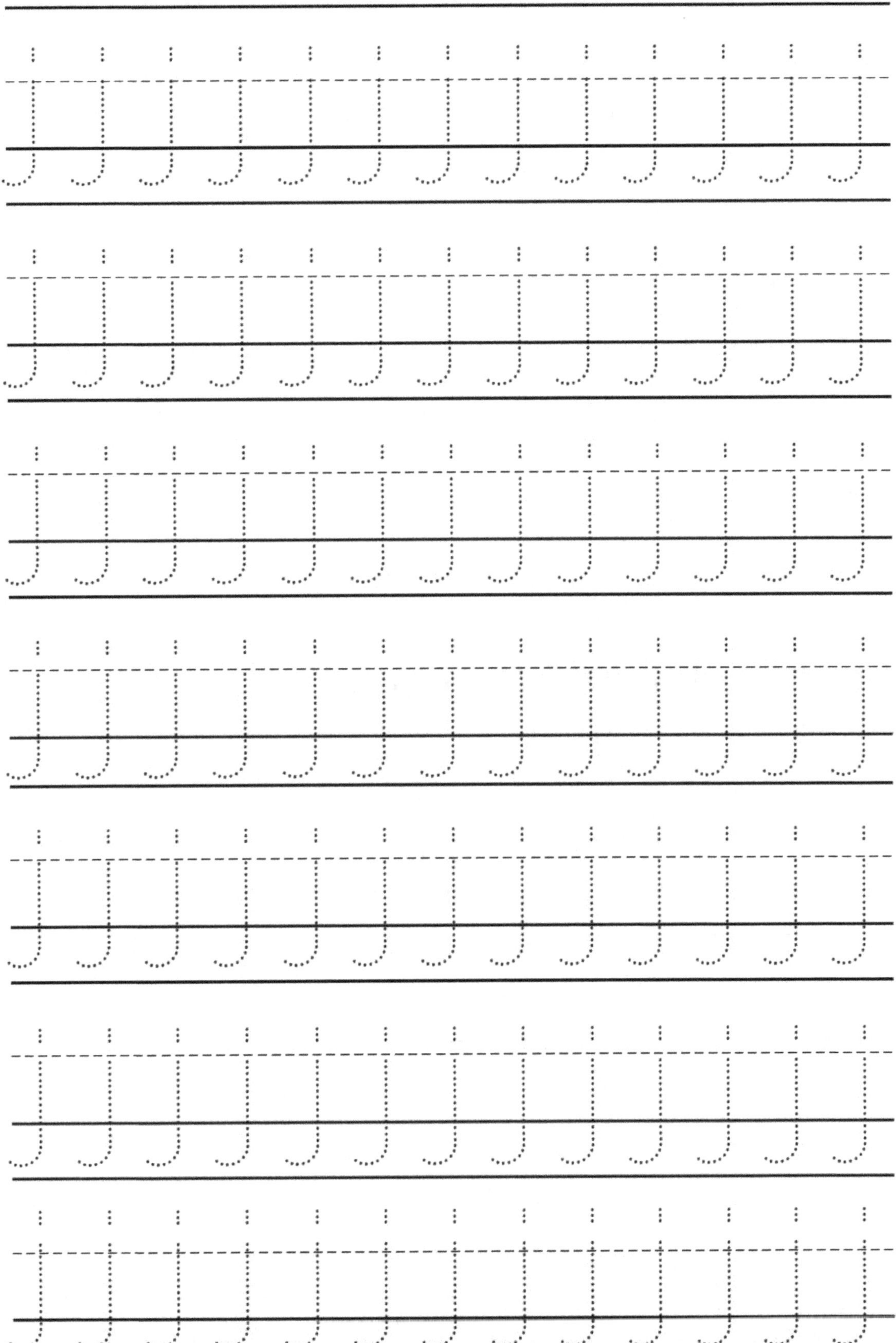

K k

Find And Circle The letter.

I	K	A	S	D	Q
P	J	K	L	N	A
W	K	T	Z	X	V
K	B	Y	I	O	A

Koala

Trace The Letter Then Write Your Own.

BE AUTHENTIC

L l

Find And Circle The letter.

L H J G I O
Q B A U L R
F S L A T Y
W T M N J L

Lobster

Trace The Letter Then Write Your Own.

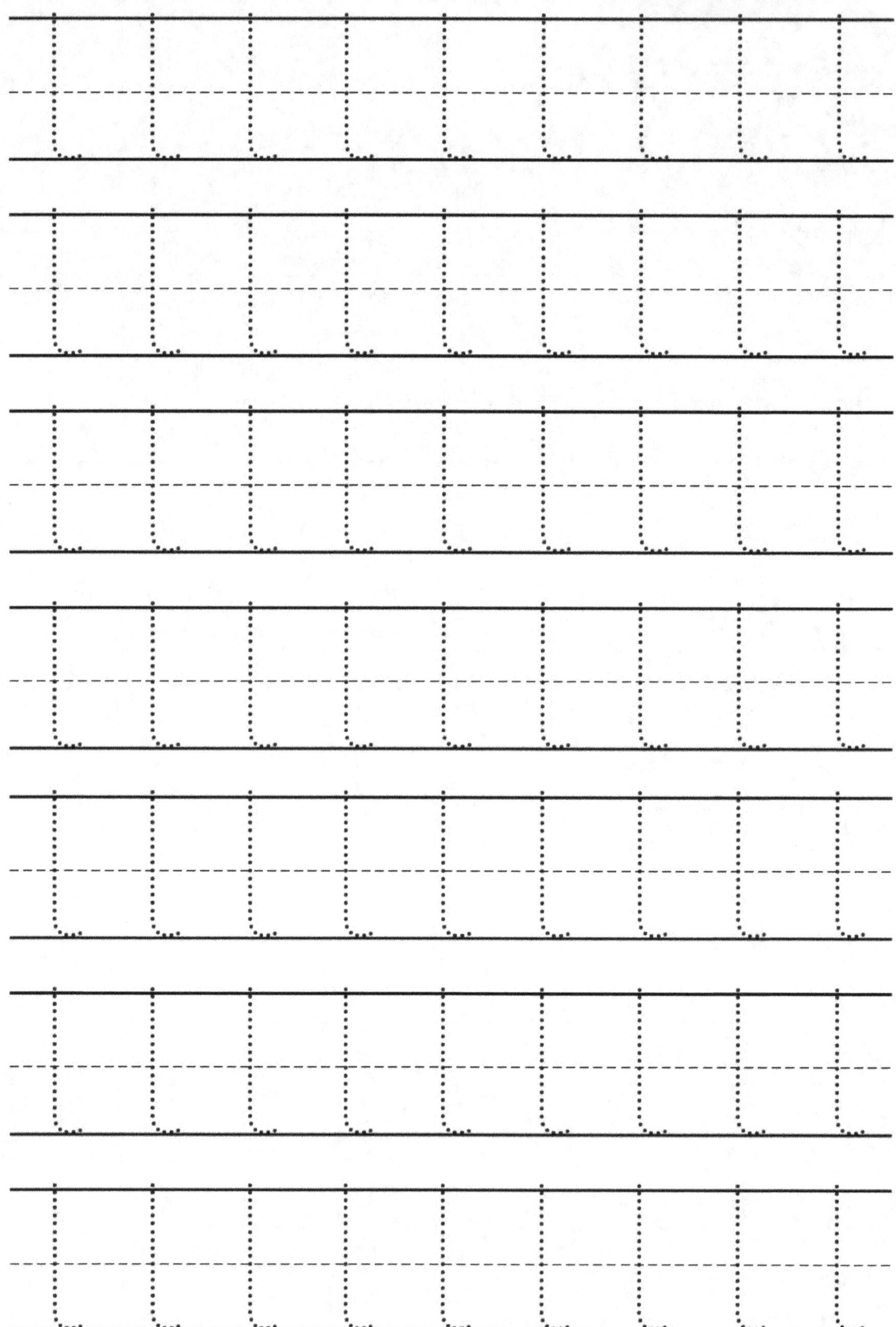

M m

Find And Circle The letter.

M	A	C	S	D	L
P	U	T	I	B	M
O	Q	M	J	K	N
Z	X	G	T	M	Y

Monkey

Trace The Letter Then Write Your Own.

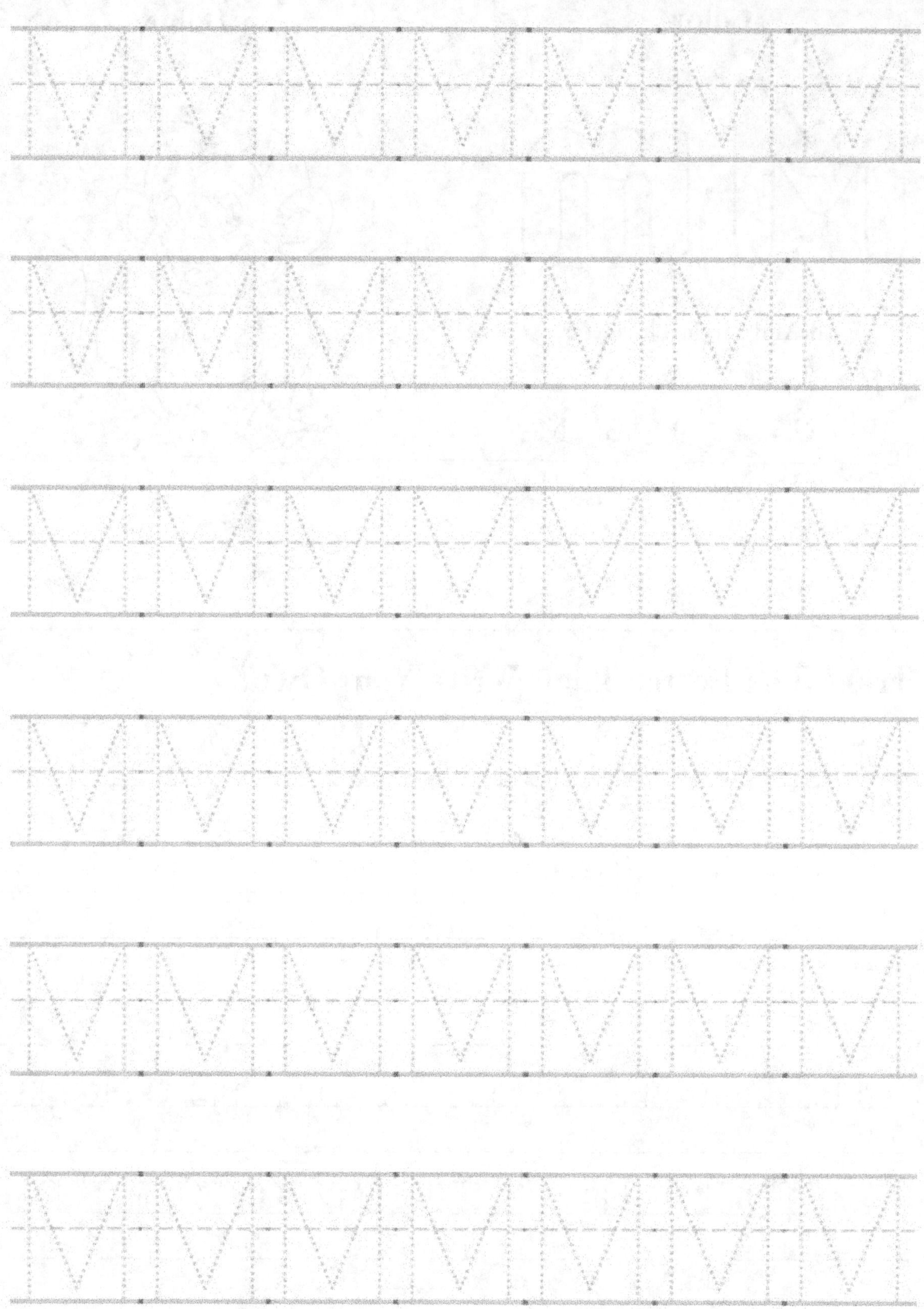

N n

Find And Circle The letter.

N	U	I	O	P	Z
S	A	N	B	M	C
F	G	H	N	J	L
K	R	T	Y	U	N

Nest

Trace The Letter Then Write Your Own.

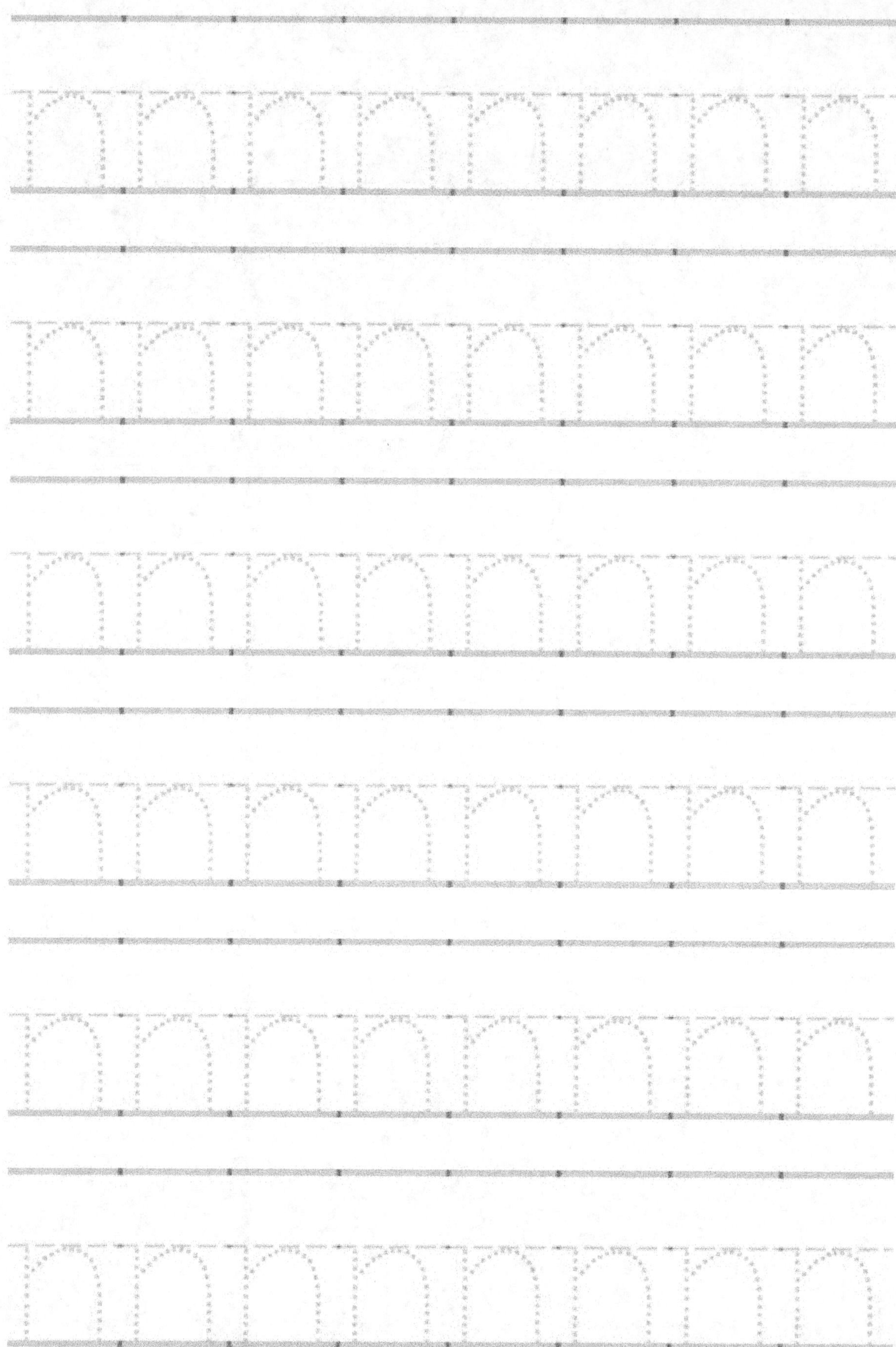

THEY ARE
ABLE
BECAUSE
THEY
THINK
THEY ARE
ABLE

Color
Color
Find And Circle The letter.
I T O U I V
S F D G O H
O J K L Z X
C V B O N A
Orange
Trace The Letter Then Write Your Own.

Color
Color

P p

Find And Circle The letter.

T	B	P	X	C	Z
L	K	J	H	P	G
P	F	D	S	E	R
B	N	P	T	A	M

Pig

Trace The Letter Then Write Your Own.

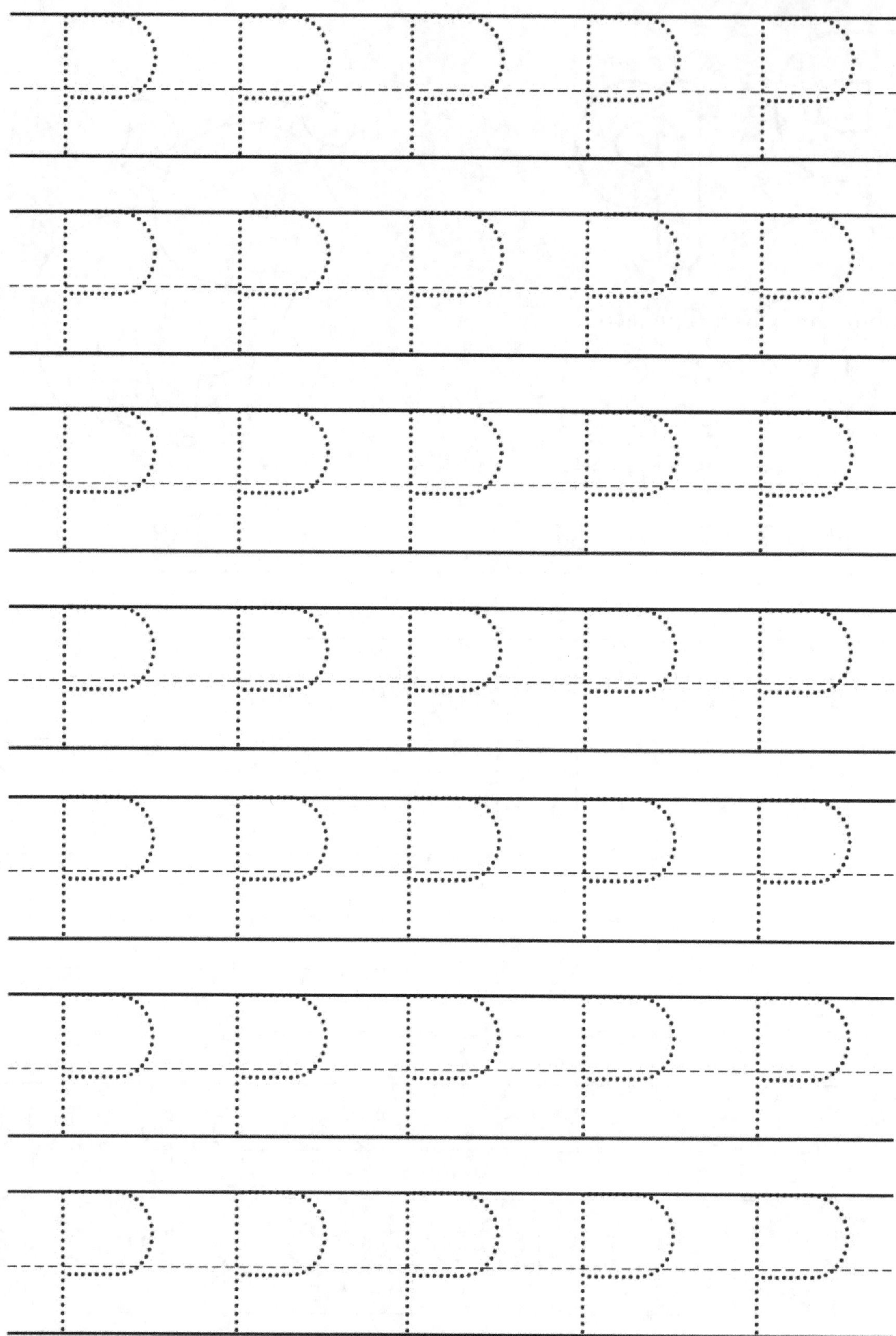

p p p p p p p p

p p p p p p p p

p p p p p p p p

p p p p p p p p

p p p p p p p p

p p p p p p p p

p p p p p p p p

Q q

Find And Circle The letter.

T	Y	U	I	L	Q
O	P	Q	L	K	J
Q	H	G	F	D	S
Z	X	C	Q	V	N

Quail

Trace The Letter Then Write Your Own.

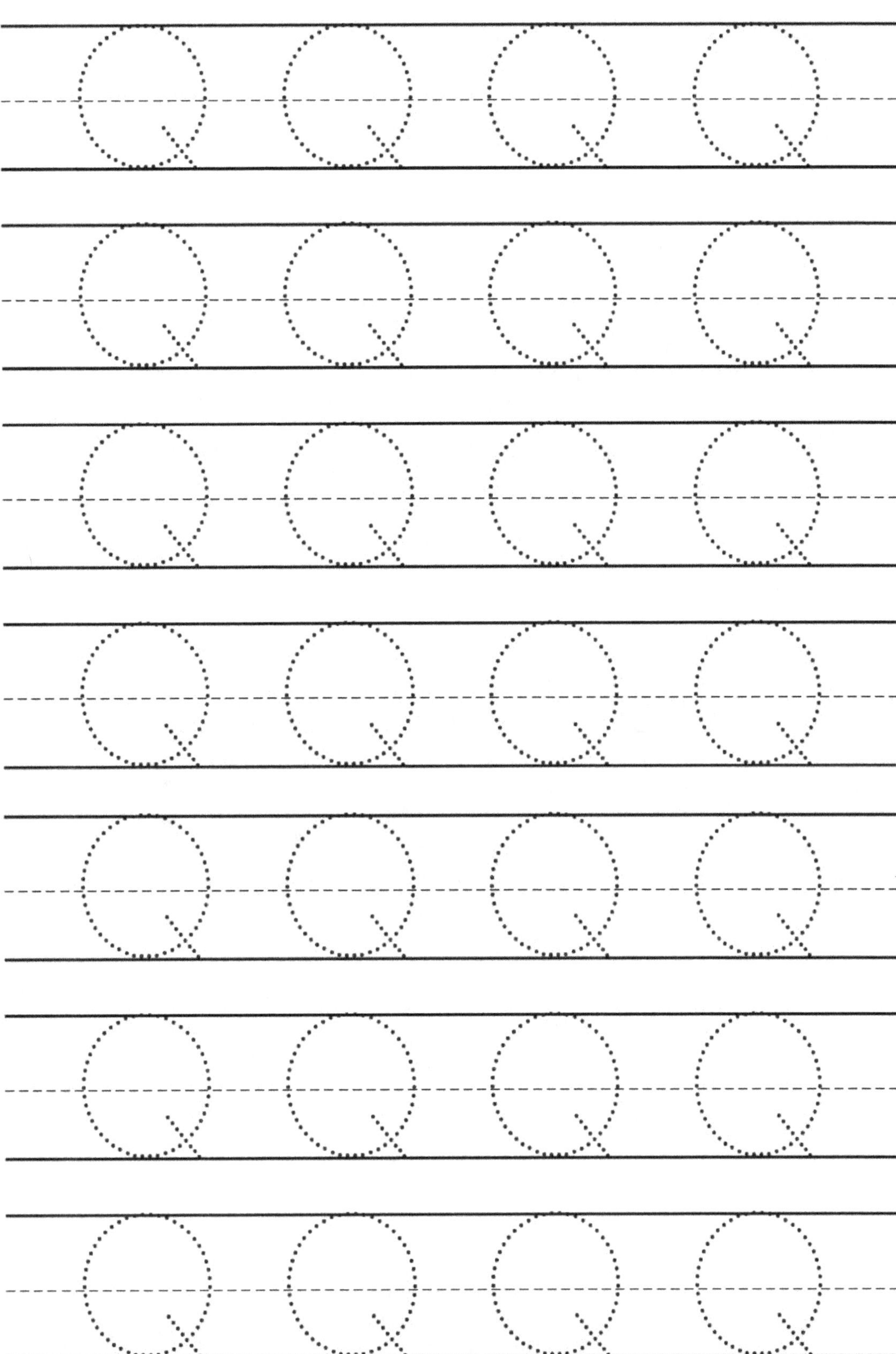

NEVER GIVE IN AND NEVER GIVE UP

R r

Find And Circle The letter.

T Y U I R O
P Q R Z S D
X C B N R M
H R J K L A

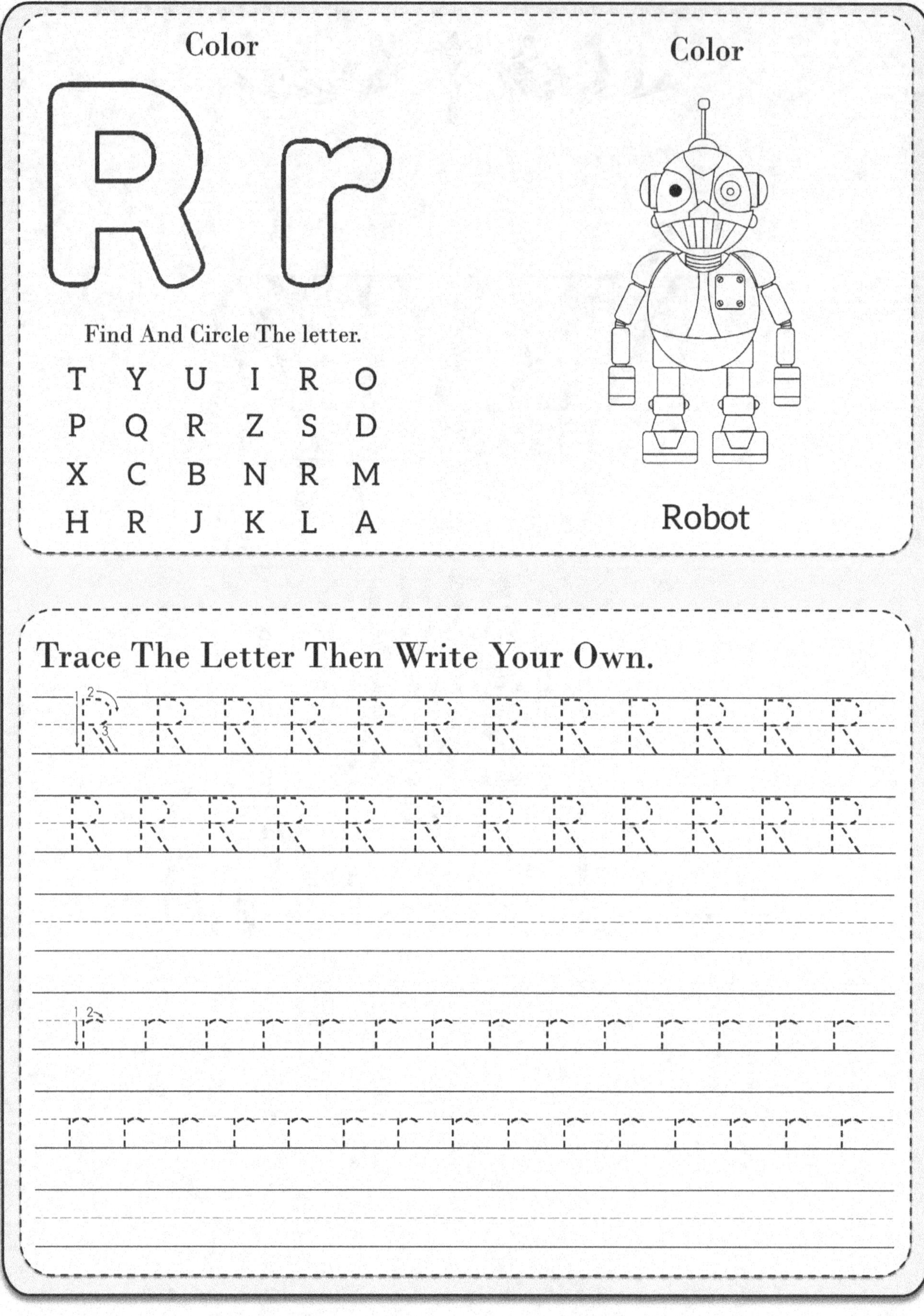

Robot

Trace The Letter Then Write Your Own.

Find And Circle The letter.

A	R	T	Y	S	B
Z	S	C	V	N	D
H	U	I	S	O	P
S	F	G	X	J	K

Snail

Trace The Letter Then Write Your Own.

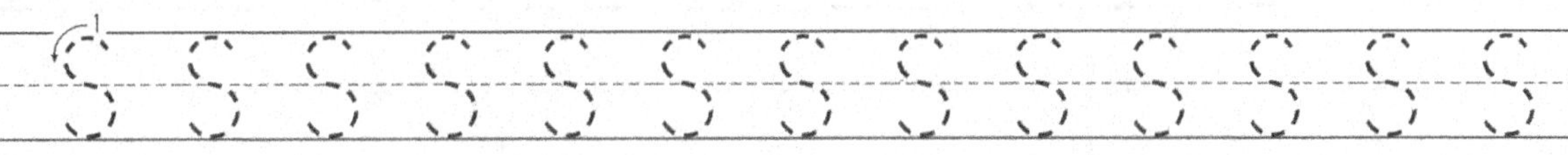

S S S S S

S S S S S

S S S S S

S S S S S

S S S S S

S S S S S

S S S S S

S S S S S S S S S

S S S S S S S S S

S S S S S S S S S

S S S S S S S S S

S S S S S S S S S

S S S S S S S S S

S S S S S S S S S

EVERY DAY IS A FRESH START

T t

Find And Circle The letter.

T	Q	W	R	E	B
S	D	F	G	H	T
J	K	L	T	Z	X
T	C	V	B	N	A

Tractor

Trace The Letter Then Write Your Own.

Trace The Letter Then Write Your Own.

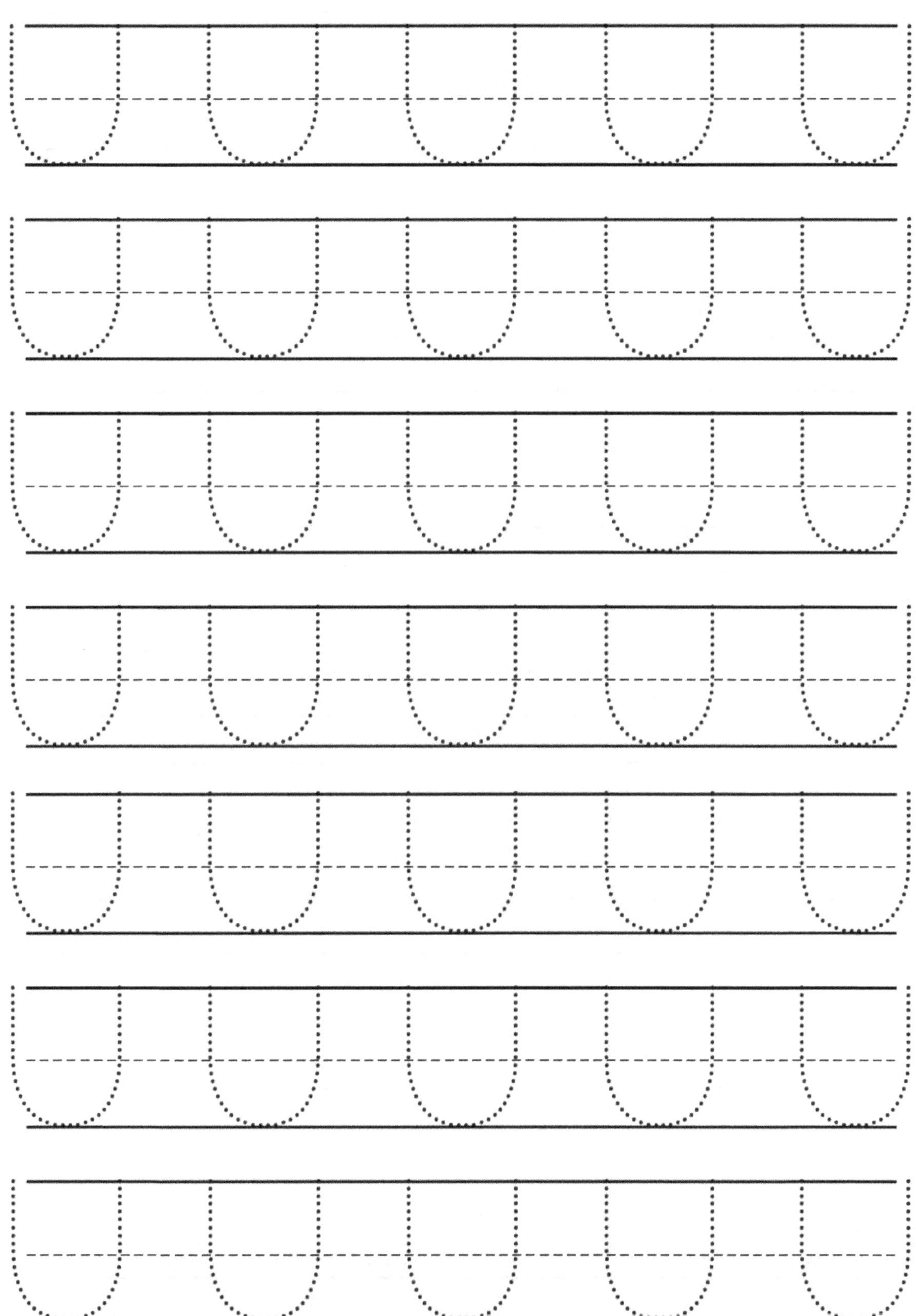

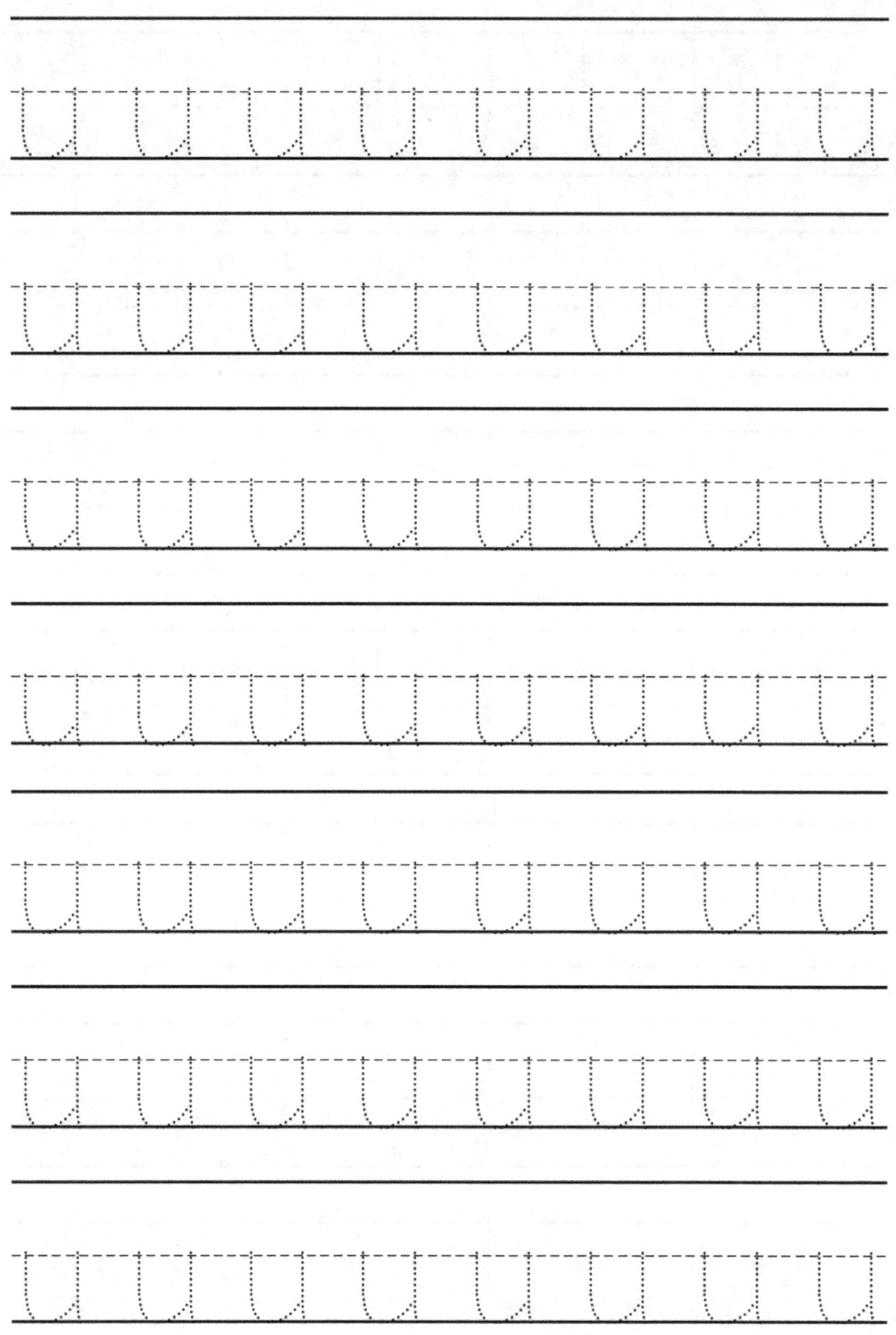

Color

Color

Find And Circle The letter.

B V Z X C N
M L K V J H
G V D F S P
O I U Y V E

Vulture

Trace The Letter Then Write Your Own.

BE NICE KID

Find And Circle The letter.

E Q R T W Y
W U I O P L
K J H W B X
Z W E F V G

Worm

Trace The Letter Then Write Your Own.

X x

Find And Circle The letter.

A X C E F D
S G H X J K
E R T Y U X
I O X P L M

Xebec

Trace The Letter Then Write Your Own.

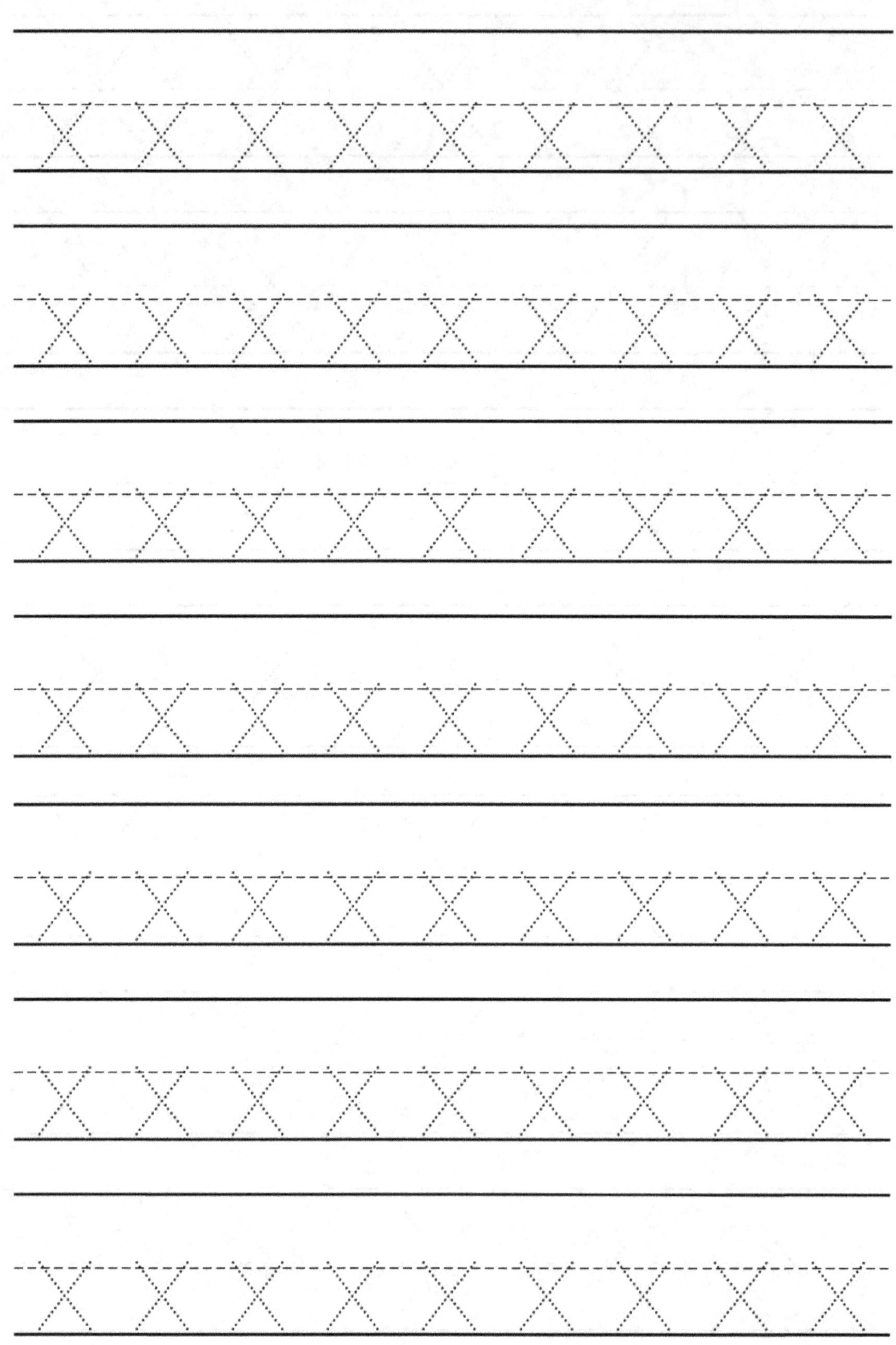

Find And Circle The letter.

Y	Q	W	E	R	T
Z	P	O	I	U	Y
X	C	Y	G	H	J
A	Y	N	B	M	L

Yarn

Trace The Letter Then Write Your Own.

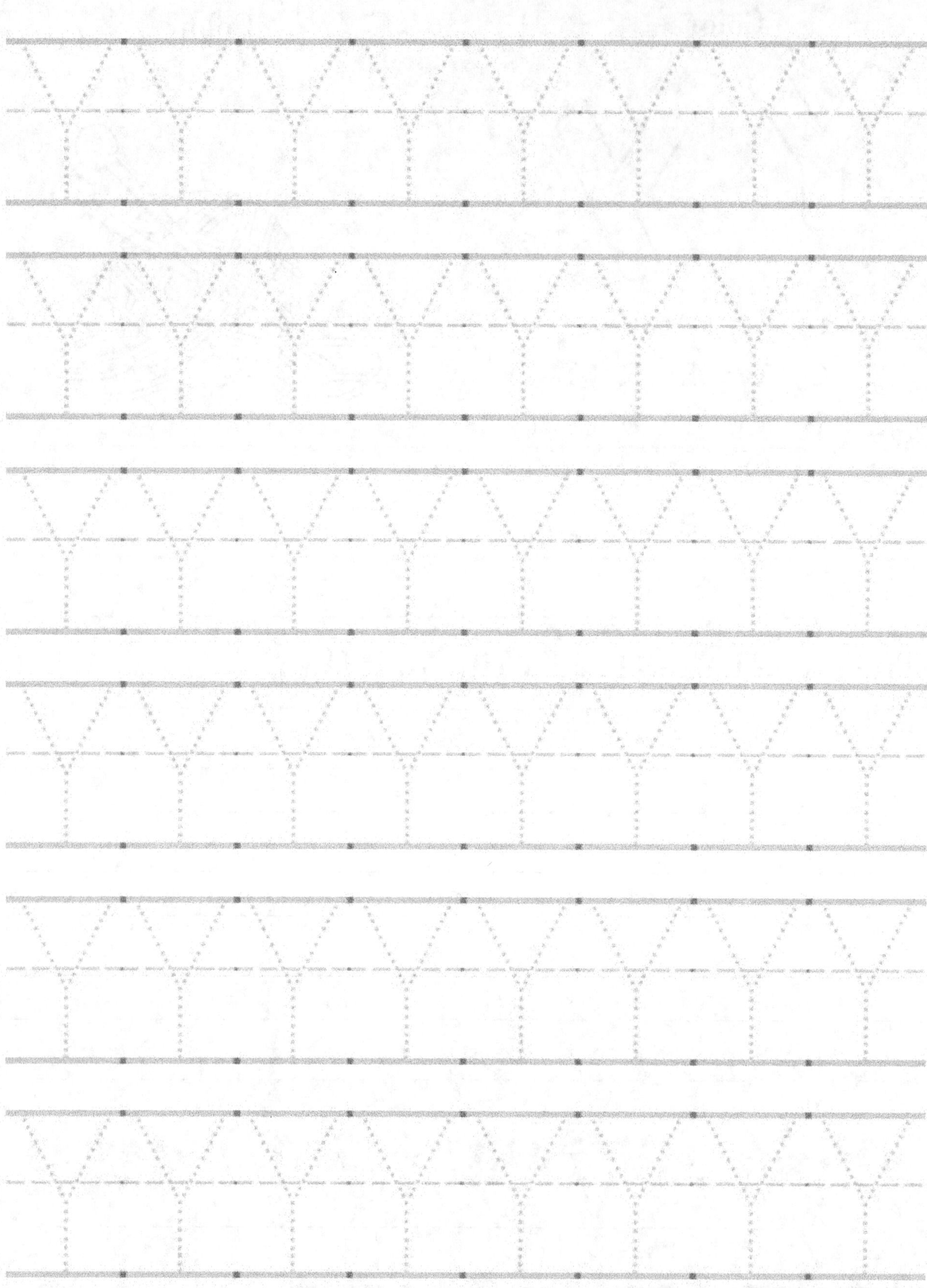

Find And Circle The letter.

Q	W	Z	E	R	T
Y	U	I	A	O	Z
S	D	F	Z	H	J
Z	X	C	B	N	K

Zeppelin

Trace The Letter Then Write Your Own.

TRACE THE LINE

Trace The Line And Practice.

TRACE THE LINE

Trace The Line And Practice.

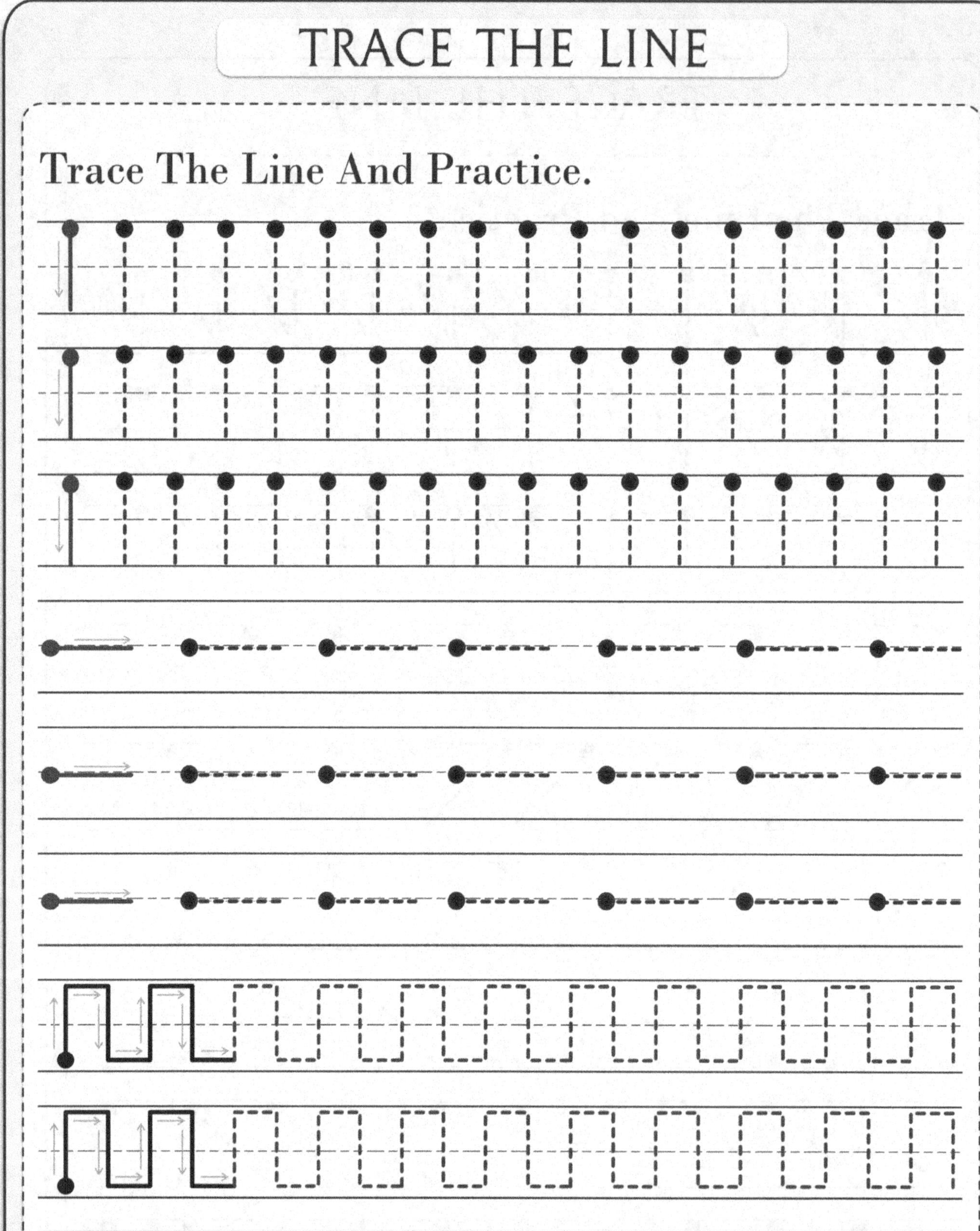

TRACE THE LINE

Trace The Line And Practice.

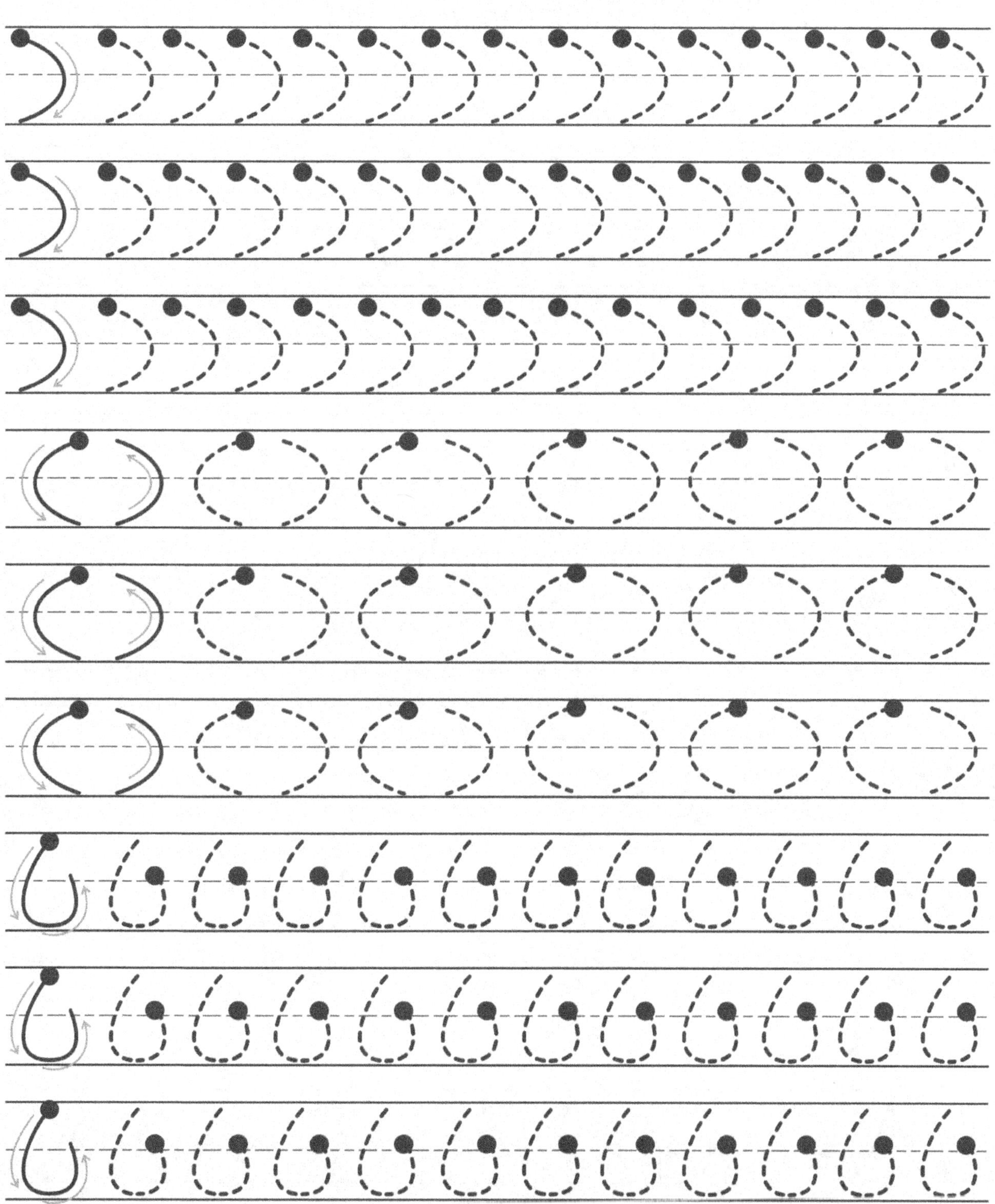

TRACE THE LINE

Trace The Line And Practice.

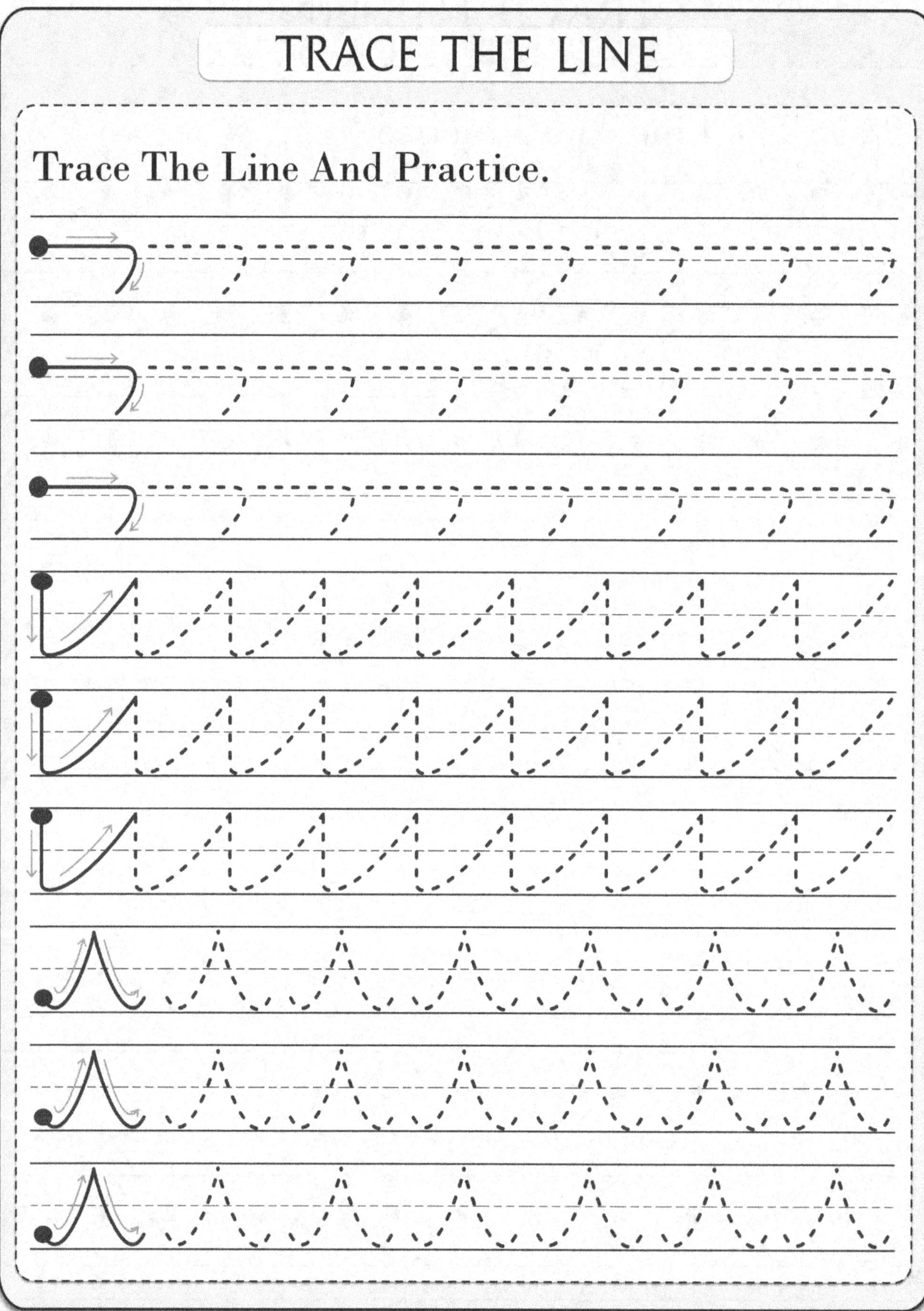

TRACE THE LINE

Trace The Line And Practice.

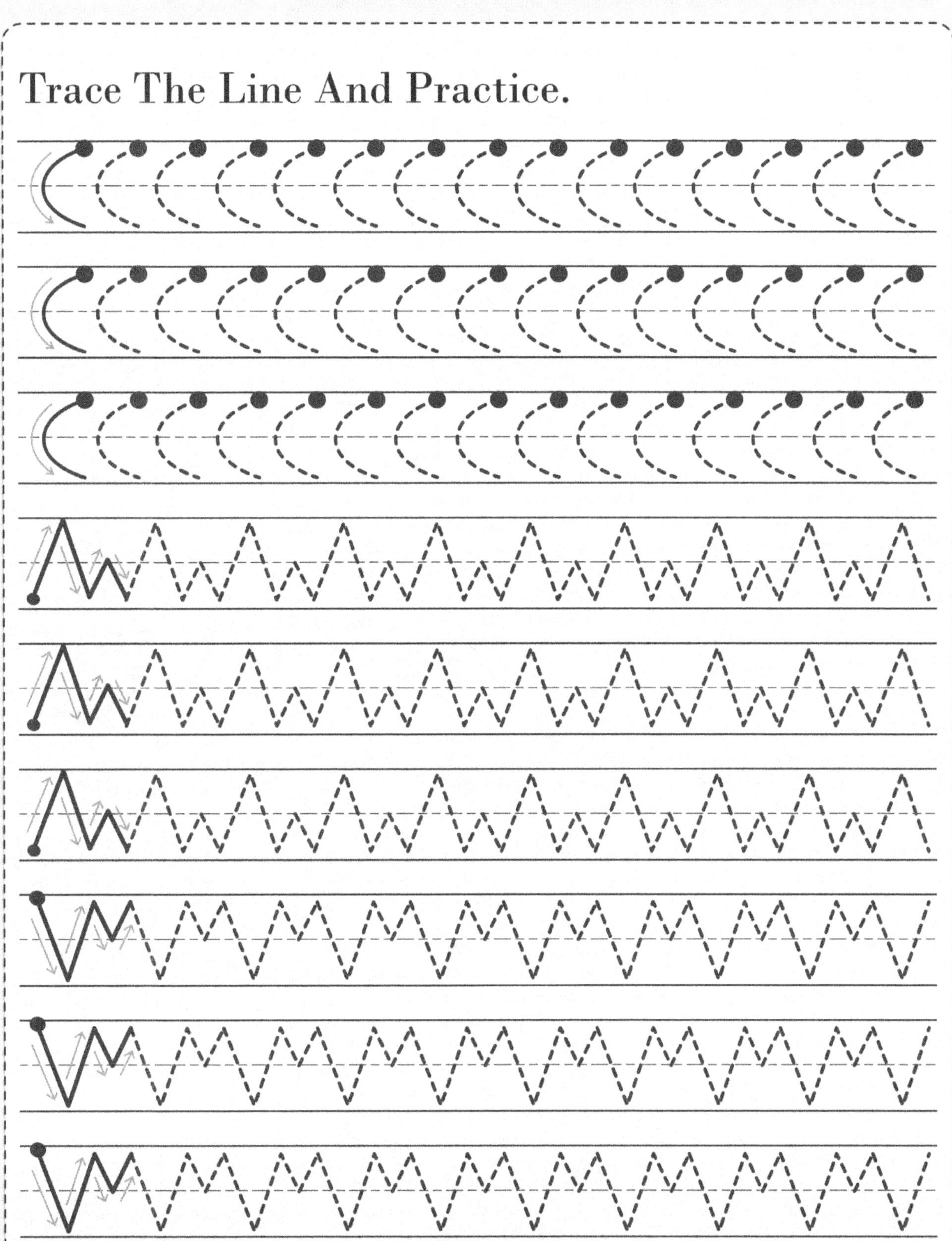